Werner Hofmann

Expressionist Watercolors

1905-1920

Harry N. Abrams, Inc. *Publishers* New York

Note

Because many readers will wish to study at their leisure some of the pictures reproduced here, the reproductions have been made detachable, and two slip-in frames have been provided (see inside back cover).

Translated by Norbert Guterman

Library of Congress Catalog Card Number: 67–25288
Published 1967 in association with Verlag M. DuMont Schauberg, Cologne
Illustrations reproduced by permission of: Cosmopress, Geneva; S.P.A.D.E.M., Paris;
A.D.A.G.P., Paris; R. N. Ketterer, Campione d'Italia; The Ada and Emil Nolde Foundation, Seebüll
All rights reserved. No part of the contents of this book may be reproduced without the written permission
of the publishers, Harry N. Abrams, Inc., New York

Printed and bound in West Germany

Contents

7 Introduction by Werner Hofmann

39 List of Watercolors and Drawings

41 Maurice de Vlaminck: *Head of Woman*, c. 1905
43 Maurice de Vlaminck: *The Village*, 1910–20.

45 John Marin: *Woolworth Building and Vicinity*, 1914
47 John Marin: *Movement—Fifth Avenue*, 1912

49 Egon Schiele: *The Artist and His Model*, 1910
51 Egon Schiele: *Sleeping Girl (The Artist's Sister Gerda)*, 1911

53 André Derain: *Barges*, 1905
55 André Derain: *Animated Landscape (Bacchanal)*, 1906

57 Otto Dix: *Man Falling*, 1918
59 Otto Dix: *House at Angres*, 1917

61 Paul Klee: *Garden Still Life with Watering Can*, 1910
63 Paul Klee: *Gardens by Night*, 1918

65 Emil Nolde: *Skaters*, 1908
67 Emil Nolde: *Stage Scene*, 1910–11

69 Marc Chagall: *Full Moon*, c. 1911
71 Marc Chagall: *Eve of Yom Kippur*, 1912

73 Erich Heckel: *Woman Resting*, 1913
75 Erich Heckel: *Seated Child*, 1910

77 Wassily Kandinsky: *Study for "Improvisation,"* 1915
79 Wassily Kandinsky: *Improvisation* 1915

81 Ernst Ludwig Kirchner: *Streetwalkers*, 1911
83 Ernst Ludwig Kirchner: *The Stübelallee* (Stübel Avenue), 1912

85 Oskar Kokoschka: *Birth of Christ*, 1910
87 Oskar Kokoschka: *Study for "Lovers with Cat,"* 1917

89 Georges Rouault: *Mau-Mau*, 1914
91 Georges Rouault: *Woman with Feathered Hat*, 1909

93 Max Ernst: *Paris Street*, 1912
95 Max Ernst: *Battling Fish*, 1917

97 Pablo Picasso: *Couple*, 1904
99 Pablo Picasso: *Brooding Woman*, 1904 (?)

101 Franz Marc: *Abstract Composition with House and Garden*, 1914
103 Franz Marc: *Three Fabulous Animals*, 1913

Marc Chagall

Pablo Picasso

Paul Klee

Wassily Kandinsky

John Marin

Emil Nolde

Oskar Kokoschka

Georges Rouault

Max Ernst

Maurice de Vlaminck

Franz Marc

André Derain

Egon Schiele

Ernst Ludwig Kirchner

Otto Dix

Erich Heckel

Picasso

EGON SCHIELE

Georges Rouault

Max Ernst

Marc Chagall

Emil Nolde

Around 1900, in discussing an Italian so-called racial tradition, the Viennese art historian Alois Riegl wrote: "The inner agitation of Italian Baroque figures strikes us Germans with our capacity for deep feeling as artificial and affected." At about the same time, unveiling a monument, the German emperor declared that "true art" is not to be confused with that other art which does not "elevate us" but "stoops to the gutter." Rising above all doubts and contradictions, the monarch went on to tell his countrymen: "For us, the German people, the great ideals have become lasting possessions, while other peoples have more or less lost sight of them." Behind this conviction it is not hard to discern another: German art, spiritually superior to foreign art, can dispense with foreign influences.

Without equating the scholar's words and the ruler's, it is yet possible to draw certain inferences as to their common intent. The scholar and the imperial arbiter of art shared a certainty that Germans are more profound, nobler, and endowed with greater inwardness than other peoples, and thereby beyond any doubt destined to higher things. The same sense of mission that determined the pseudo style of Wilhelmian power politics also left its imprint on the kind of poetry and art that appeals to the Philistine and the cultivated burgher.

It would be a mistake, however, to limit the aspiration to "greater depth, imagination, soulfulness"—words used by the artless Carl Vinnen when he referred to "the special characteristics of our people" in his *Protest deutscher Künstler* (1911)—to the common or garden variety of emotional cliché. The aspiration has a deeper, older origin, and its effects reach further, though they are by no means all of a piece. It is better viewed as symptomatic of a general receptivity groping for orientation; stemming from different sources of malaise and frustration, it is shared by almost all strata of society. Since each of these strata associates its wish for "greater depth" with other longings, other expectations relating to form and content, the artistic responses to it, too, lead to different modes of expression, and the latter in turn differ in value. They range from nationalist to ancient mythology, from unworldly inwardness to the optimistic "spring awakening" of the *Jugendstil*, from trivial art to esoteric symbolism. Among them we find works by Thomas, Menzel, Böcklin, Klinger, and Marées.

Expressionism is another of these responses, although it speaks a different language. Considering the depth of experience of which its artists boasted, it is not surprising that the moment it appeared on the scene it became a controversial topic in the debate on national self-determination in the domain of the spirit. It was singled out by friend and foe alike for putting to the test philosophical slogans that often sounded much the same. The artists themselves—though not all of them—were innocent enough to offer nationalistic or folkloric arguments in self-justification. That Nolde, just like Böcklin, held a low opinion of French art is well known. The *Chronik* of the *Brücke* (1913) proudly asserts that the group stood in direct line of descent from the art of the German Middle Ages and owed nothing whatever to foreign influences. It proclaims its goal to be a "human culture," which alone "is the soil in which a real art can grow." Although the group's theoreticians spoke in terms of "humanity," they were ready to fall back on the argument of national peculiarity. There is something a bit presumptuous in the claim to

7

autarchy, also in the conviction that by virtue of its universality the aspiration to "real art" must make it superior to "merely artistic" foreign movements. The *Chronik* mentions Cubism and Futurism.

And yet, despite the attempts by artists and followers to keep it local and national, the Expressionist movement was centrifugal in its effects. Although as late as the thirties some Expressionists were still trying to prove their North German ancestry—a tactic that did not spare them from defamation by the new rulers—the adversaries of Expressionism both then and earlier had different ideas as to what constitutes a "characteristic national art." The judgment of conservative and reactionary critics is spoiled by sheer contempt, but it does contain one correct observation concerning the origin of Expressionism. When the artists who were gathered together in Munich's Neue Künstlervereinigung included a few Paris Fauves in their exhibitions, conservative critics charged the Germans (among whom were not a few Russians) with aping the "clowning" of a few French artists not taken very seriously even in Paris. "They apparently think they can impress the German public by calling upon their Paris prototypes as evidence of the fact that they are not lagging behind the most modern of the French."

The scoffer was right when he stressed the leading part played by the French. His judgment is further confirmed by the fact that the term "Expressionists" was first applied to French, not German painters. We find this designation in the catalogue of the twenty-second exhibition of the Berlin "Secession" (1911), applied to a number of French painters who exhibited in a separate hall. These earliest "Expressionists" were mostly Fauves: Marquet, Puy, Vlaminck, Manguin, Van Dongen, Derain—and Picasso. Fritz Schmalenbach conjectures that the term "was coined then and there for that exhibition; however, the public assumed (and certainly was encouraged to do so) that the name was in current use in France to designate those painters."

II

Though the old question whether Expressionism should be looked upon as a German or an international phenomenon has been removed from the plane of polemics, it has still to be answered. To "nationalize" Expressionism is to cut off its full range of influence and, moreover, to expose it to the critical eye of Romance language prejudice (which exists no less than the Germanic). To take the opposite course, as we are doing in this volume, is to run the risk of blurring boundary lines. What it is most important to avoid, perhaps, is too academic a definition of Expressionism. The term may well be at once too narrow and too broad to provide a clear-cut basis for understanding the artistic phenomena involved. If Expressionism is defined primarily as a challenge to positivism and materialism, then it could be argued that Cubism and Futurism belong under the same heading. Franz Marc, for instance, must have taken it in this broad sense when—no doubt without realizing it—he read his own creative intentions into a Cubist picture by Picasso, praising it for making visible the "mystical inward construction" in the world-image of the era.

Art history has not been able to disentangle the skein of shadowy meanings that have grown up around the term. The historian's predilection for neatly opposed simplifications—we may recall that Wölfflin's

8

JOHN MARIN (PHOTO 1945) ▷

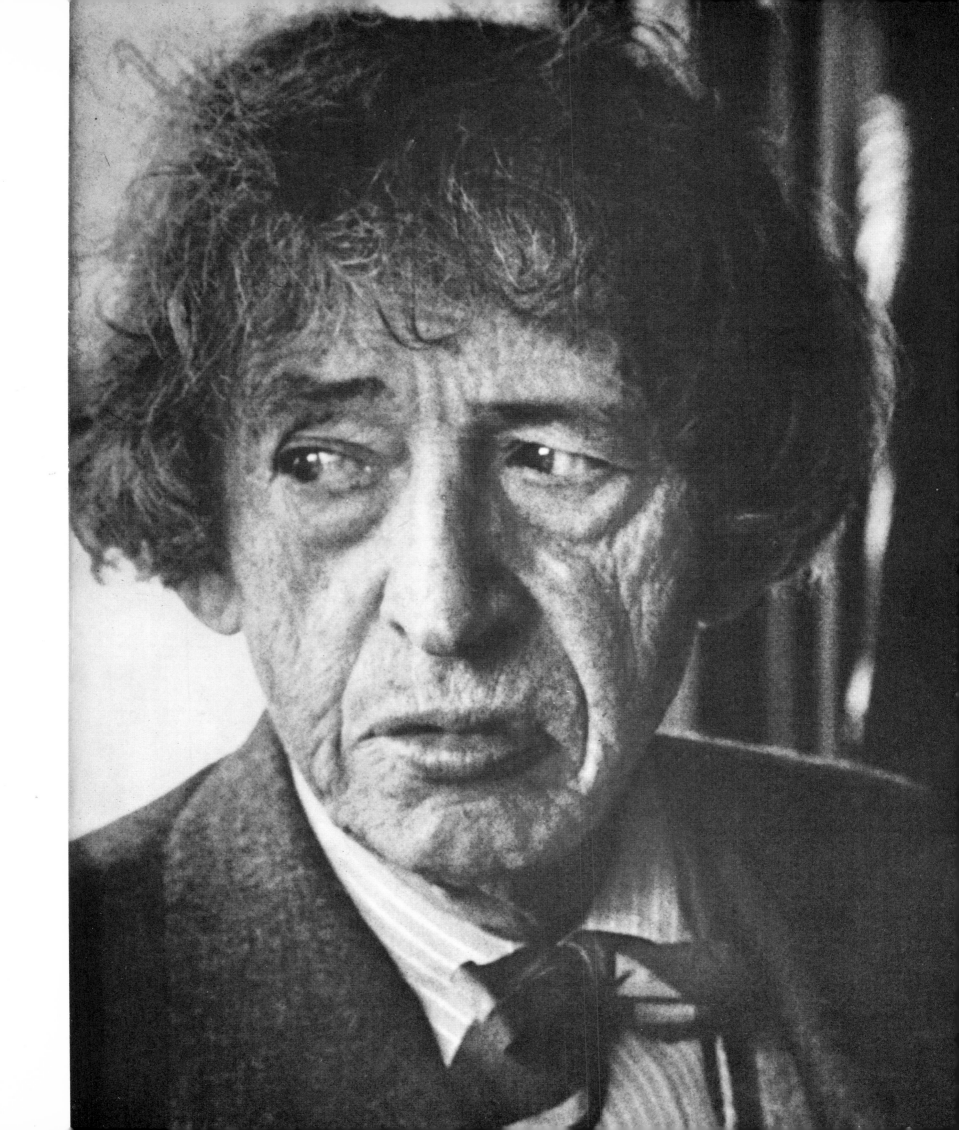

Grundbegriffe (Principles of Art History) appeared in 1915—found in Expressionism a welcome pretext for speculation. It all seemed perfectly clear: With truly Hegelian consequence the Romance language joy in living had to be replaced with the disembodied spirituality of the Germanic tradition; the "soulless" imitation of nature had to give way to unchecked domination by the psychic. Nor, as we shall see, are the other clichés more tenable. To clear away the idealistic commonplaces that have accumulated around "Expressionism"—a label, unfortunately, we cannot do without—it is necessary first of all to set aside the more ponderous theoretical glosses. We are disregarding such insights as the antithesis between "depth" and "surface," the guaranteed nobility of "inwardness," and the stigma of "barbaric formlessness"—the whole conceptual apparatus of academic criticism. Instead, we shall try to engage the pictures in direct dialogue.

Anyone who is even cursorily aware of the formal range the phenomenon "Expressionism" presents—the reproductions in this volume should suffice—will note that it allows of more variation than Cubism or Futurism. Our present selections, in but a single technique—watercolor—run the gamut between two poles. At one extreme, emphasis lies on the attractions of the primary act of handwriting, as represented in the watercolors by Derain, Kandinsky, Kirchner, Kokoschka, Marin, Nolde, Picasso, and Rouault. At the other extreme, the artists have striven for meticulous pictorial form and consolidation, tempering the wealth of changes the medium offers to intuitive freedom, taming spontaneous immediacy, and bringing the watercolor close to a finished painting, sometimes with the intervention of gouache. This second group includes the painterly watercolors by Chagall, Dix, Ernst, Heckel, Klee, Marc, Schiele, and Vlaminck. However, we must take into account the fact that many works in the first group, too, are so to speak in the antechamber of oil painting. Kokoschka's *Lovers with Cat* (p. 87) was his linear-rhythmic study for a painting today in the Zurich Kunsthaus. And like his *Animated Landscape* (p. 55), Derain's Fauve oils often make use of the effects the white ground offers, to bring out the juxtaposed unmixed colors with greater intensity. Kandinsky and Marin both were accustomed to using first the small format, then transferring onto canvas the space ordered by merging planes and sweeping lines. As for Rouault, between 1905 and 1910 watercolor represented a means of expression directly preparatory to oil painting.

For this reason we should note carefully one important characteristic of the Expressionist watercolor. Even where its effect is highly elementary, scarcely more than the rough blocking out of a pictorial idea, it does not have the purely provisional character of a sketch made on the run. Its formal character makes higher claims, bespeaks a creative impulse directed toward the bold, vital act of painting. The artist attempts to reach his goal by the shortest possible route, rarely betrays the slightest hesitation, and almost never makes corrections later. The approach might be defined more accurately as a kind of interaction—the boundaries between the two mediums are overstepped in both directions, so that watercolor and oil painting enhance each other. Trained in the economy of expression that watercolor encourages, the brushwork in oil painting gains speed and, thereby, formal and chromatic concentration. At the same time, the watercolorist is enabled to endow his "private," traditionally less "serious" statement with a more "public" resonance, gaining in independence and decisiveness. In short, the Expressionist endows the fugitive charms of transparent watercolor with something of monumental power.

10

III

The rich range of variation exhibited by Expressionist artists goes back to the historical sources. Linking up Gauguin's search for an earthly paradise with Van Gogh's throbbing brushstroke, Derain and Kirchner continued the violent dramatization of elemental color experiences such as the Impressionists had been first to wrest from nature. The expansive spot of color takes on its maximal measure of quicksilvery life and vital pleasure when paired with another.

The American John Marin, too, was influenced by Impressionism, though he did not begin by celebrating the idyllic luxuriance of landscape. Rather, he began with the tectonic axial structure of the cityscape. This was his background when he discovered Cézanne's art in 1911. To it he owes his way of achieving gradations of space with transparent prismatic planes of color; he may also owe to Cézanne his resolve to break up his formal structures dynamically. If the Fauves learned from Cézanne how to come to terms with form and make it a stronger element—Vlaminck's *The Village* (p. 43) is a case in point—Marin discovered in him the possibilities of dematerialization. It seems that, although he lived in Paris until the summer of 1911, he knew nothing about the way the Cubists were splintering form, nor about Futurist visions of the big city. The first Futurist exhibition in Paris was not held until February, 1912, by which time Marin was back in New York and had begun, probably without reference to any pictorial model, his series of skyscraper visions (pp. 45 and 47).

Whereas Van Gogh broke away from the Impressionists' delicate tracery of interwoven colors and created his own rough but rich brushstroke calligraphy, Gauguin attempted rather to condense color in flat areas enclosed in luminous monochrome islands. More restful areas of color were consistently raised to a higher power in Nolde's *Stage Scene* (p. 67) and in Heckel's *Seated Child* (p. 75), i. e., they were enlarged and barbarized. The ornamental qualities of line such as Gauguin had cultivated were now sacrificed. In Nolde, outlines are blurred with the glowing colors, and in Heckel, they are relegated to a still more modest role.

Other painters were particularly drawn to the highly disciplined linearism that came into vogue at the close of the nineteenth century. Even Derain let himself be seduced by the gracefulness of curving plant-like arabesques, and skillfully exploited their unifying effect. Rouault fairly flings his lines at the paper in virtuoso whiplashes, the lambent nervous movement of which derives from Toulouse-Lautrec but aspires to even bolder, more impulsive renderings of the human body's twists and turns. In Rouault the sudden spots of color that flare up are independent of the linear rhythm.

The kind of Expressionism practiced by Kokoschka and Schiele goes back to Klimt's noble *Jugendstil* line. Kokoschka was quick to weary of this devotion to line, however, and began to churn up his lines, alternately tangling and untangling them until he had got back to their chaotic origins and learned how to reconcile the tension between line and color in an impetuous interlacing of brushstrokes. The figures

12

in his *Lovers with Cat* (p. 87) are constructed of a cluster of colored lines, a model for which is to be found in the pre-Baroque Tintoretto. In the meantime, Schiele was wresting from the linear grid a melancholy metaphor expressive of loneliness, too disciplined to permit blurring with color and renouncing a spontaneous, quick-sketch, roughly approximate line (p. 51).

Side by side with bravura treatment of line, the turn of the century was preoccupied also with how forms blend passively and nebulously flit away, expressing states between dream and waking. Redon, Carrière, Munch, and the Nabis exploited this twilight world to produce a poetry of solitude, which also imparts its fathomless spell to Picasso's *Brooding Woman* (p. 99).

In the differently articulated impulses characterizing this first Expressionist wave it is possible to find a basis for distinguishing a second wave. To borrow a term from linguistics, what happened was a sort of vowel shift brought about by the appearance of Cubism and Futurism. The central feature of this second wave may be described as follows: The effervescent dynamism of the pictorial structure is tightened up, becomes angular or jagged, is pervaded with basically geometric figures. The interlocking, overlapping complexes of form so produced are distributed among different domains of expression. When Chagall hardens his pictorial elements and endows them with sharply angular outlines, he does this as a rule to test the ciphers of his archaic narrative mode. Marc interlaces animals, trees, and stars to form an acute-angled "cathedral" (p. 103) with the aid of Cubist-Futurist formal signals. Klee invents a labyrinthine tapestry of flat surfaces—"a felt geometry"—within which our slowly groping gaze is wholly swallowed up. Kandinsky is a special case. From his Fauve phase he passed in 1910 to a radical dispersal of the closed form. He condemns stylized, ornamental, experimental forms (the manuscript of a 1914 lecture tells us about this), and yet resorts to lightning-fast axes of orientation whose throbs, dislocations, and collisions now and again bring to mind the Futurists' repertory of "jagged" forms (p. 79).

The watercolors by Dix and Ernst show the expressive potentialities of interlocking, interlacing forms; on the one hand, this is to take possession of tangible reality, on the other, to make a joking commentary on the mystique of cosmic unity. Dix reintroduces the diagonal spatial axes of the Futurists into the world of experience. In the chaos and ravages of war he demonstrates the actual consequences of those orgies of destruction which Marinetti and his circle had celebrated at a time when Europe was still at peace. By contrast, Ernst employs the vocabulary of the *Blaue Reiter* to invent a polyvalent world of fable, impelled by mysterious mechanisms, which brings Bosch and Bruegel to mind (pp. 59 and 95).

These briefly sketched insights into the multiplicity of possible Expressionist idioms open up two paths for further investigation. One might lead to examining the different strata of expression through a critical differentiation of styles, concentrating on influences, interrelations, chronological sequence, and specific local features. The other might lead to a search for common elements. The former properly demands a detailed historical study, but the latter can be attempted, at least in rough outline, within the framework of an essay. The central theme of our reflections, then, will be: Is there a point where the different Ex-

14

OTTO DIX (PHOTO 1912) ▷

pressionisms meet? Is there—in the domain of verbal interpretation—at least *one* formula that applies to all?

IV

In 1910—an especially fruitful year in the history of art—Klee painted his *Garden Still Life with Watering Can* (p. 61). On a sheet no bigger than the palm of one's hand, a number of objects are recognizable: at lower right a fragment of trellis, then a bucket, a watering can, a bench, and in the back, apart from the domain of things and their shadows, a light wall leading diagonally into depth. So bald an enumeration leaves out the watercolor's crucial feature: Although we make out these things, they are not perceived as delimited. The eye sees, not distinct details, but interlocking zones of color along which it moves, touching object-elements, passing through them, and leaving them behind. The eye takes in the entire picture surface in a single gliding movement, never losing sight of the colored landscape that guides it and never running into an unbridgeable boundary. Starting at the top left, for instance, it follows the brownish strip of ground and the bench to where the latter slopes away, and then feels its way down to the domain of shadows along a thin rod. It is received by a cool velvety dimness. This field of shadows is more than mere accompaniment to its object. It unfolds a life of its own and can become an object. Suddenly and all of a piece, out of the shaded blue, the outline of a watering can emerges. In this way a remarkable change of meaning is effected in the color: Only a moment before it was a metaphor for darkness with no link to any material, whereas now, though there has been no qualitative change, it denotes a tangible object standing in the light. The eye keeps on moving farther to the right, finding it easy to leave the watering can. Taking advantage of the blue surface which now turns again into shadow, the eye is confronted with the alternative of following the rim of the bucket or of traveling upward into gradually darkening zones of color.

At no point is this optical journey interrupted by a formal caesura. Everything in the picture is in direct communication with everything else. It is as though they breathed with each other's breath, as though they had saturated each other with their color so that their edges are obliterated and only the overall rhythm is left. Just as none of the objects leads a life of its own, so their symbiotic configuration cannot be separated from the rest of the picture surface. On the contrary, figure and ground are firmly held together. The landscape, for the most part blue, which our eye tried to follow, is bound with surprising tightness to the light ground. It is no accident that the watering can, and the area of shadow next to it, all impinge on the pale yellow surface of the wall. Once we have noticed that the spout of the watering can is an eye, the "nose" (nozzle) of the can pointing to the right immediately encourages further association, and we begin to make out a profile. As though to confirm the dialogue between the light and the dark pictorial elements, another eye surrounded by shadow responds to the "eye" of the watering can. A dialogue begins—the half of the face in light looks different from the half in dark. Both combine in a glance at once questioning and filled with intense surprise, directed half inward, half outward to the world. The mystery of this gaze lies in the unequal pair of eyes—a feature that will recur throughout this painter's work.

17

◁ PAUL KLEE (PHOTO: COURTESY FELIX KLEE)

The watercolor contains three layers of meaning, to which three domains of form correspond. Language cannot express adequately the way these zones flow continuously into one another. There is the layer that informs us about things. To be sure, the information we get cannot be said to be objectively unambiguous—it would hardly satisfy the curiosity of a positivist. And yet it is precisely therein that the poetic magic of this metamorphosis of reality lies. Hypertrophied complexes of planes are growing out from the objects and only remotely suggest objective contents. This is the second layer, inseparable from the first, indeed fused with it. Here the link with the world of things referred to in the title is loosened. We slowly discover that we are being presented with a vast residue of potential meanings, and we are learning how to explore it. Those who take advantage of this opportunity reach the third layer. Out of the no man's land of forms, out of an objective inventory that has now become uncertain, transitory, a new "figure" suddenly emerges—a face made of light and dark, which radiates a spell-binding power. Our own gaze is as though swallowed up, submerged in, become identical with the gaze of the things—it is as though we were looking at them with their own eyes.

V

Klee noted in the catalogue he kept of his works that the watercolor was painted from nature. To many a viewer, supposing this to be a product of imagination based on visual impressions, the clue will seem important. Whenever a picture of nature, the outdoors, is in question, we tend to think of Impressionist landscapes, and we should not overlook their historical contribution. The Impressionist way of painting was rooted in a democratic, open, conciliatory vision of the world. These painters would not let anything appear in their pictures as proudly self-sufficient, as separate and distinct. Everything was brought into harmony with everything else and, at the same time, brought to the same level. A man, i. e., an aggregate of spots of color, was no more or less important than a house or a cloud. Softened at the edges, living creatures and things were brought into intimate association with one another, with their own shadows, with their surroundings. There are no individual phenomena, only a homogeneous color/light continuum woven together in short brushstrokes. Not unless we are fully aware of the equalizing effect of the all-embracing harmony supplied by the texture of the brushstrokes in Impressionist and Pointillist painting are we capable of grasping how far Klee has come in this little watercolor with its symbiosis of forms. To explain the shift in emphasis is to retrace the path leading from the Impressionists to the Expressionists.

The Impressionists applied the idea of external fusion to the contents of perception. Light was supposed to link all phenomena with one another, to assimilate the hard to the soft, the near to the distant, the animate to the inanimate. And light does perform this transforming task, but there are limits to how much it can do. Even where the Impressionist cult of light transfigures things, divesting them of their material compactness, it leaves intact their objective existence. The Impressionist does not deform. Even though his is not a meticulous description of the world of objects, he yet preserves its empirically familiar basic features.

Klee refused to be guided by the perceptive process of what Ruskin called "the innocent eye." He does not comply with the physiological law. He was, however, quite familiar with the freedoms the Impres-

sionists had won for painting. He makes use of them and adds new ones. The formal process has now become conscious, has taken on a greater degree of autonomy. Having come of age, color can either disso-ciate itself from the world of things or flow back into it again. It can be lured into adventures on its own, be driven into uncertain no man's lands where, absolved of all obligations, it is entirely its own master. Abstractly speaking, Klee uses color as a heuristic principle. (Needless to say, this is also true of his use of line, but that does not concern us here.) It is this confidence in the power of the artistic means to make their own discoveries and inventions that makes the Expressionist. Not over-concerned with the actual properties of the objective world, he reveals a greater confidence in the artistic means than the Im-pressionists displayed.

Did Klee deliberately choose to paint the strip of ground across the picture in the color we ascribe to water, or was he guided by his impression of the scene? The world he proposes to us has the consistency of a fluid, can be read only in its transitions: it never exactly *is*, but changes continuously. To show this visually, no technique is more suitable than watercolor. What is the nature of this flowing, what impulses determine it? We saw that the contact of a thing with its shadow produces a new thing, and that the latter in turn strikes out in various directions or takes shelter in larger islands of form. What began with groping, impromptu brush movements is transformed into sympathetic relationships of giving and receiv-ing, outflow and inflow, coupling and fertilization. One thing is obvious—this harmony is not externally ordained. As with the Impressionists, it derives from color, but this color is not the reflection of light falling uniformly over the world, but a substance that belongs to the object. It emerges from them, sends out antennae, gives rise to surprising dialogues, mixes up the animate with the inanimate, and in the end becomes a fluid aura whose force of attraction is active among the things themselves. Everything is assumed to be potentially soluble, nothing is permanent or solid. The objects are containers whose chromatic contents spill over their outlines.

The result is a kind of coexistence very different from what we get in an Impressionist picture. The objects are not imbedded in a uniform color-grid or assimilated to one another by being reduced to some least common denominator. Klee's symbiosis of forms treats the data of perception far more freely, conferring meaningful accents upon them. Although the individual form is tightly linked to a large domain and cannot be set off from it, it is given higher value and new dignity. Whereas in the Impressionist brush stroke structure it had regressed to the role of a mere color indicator, it now takes on a prominence that arrests the eye, challenges it, perturbs it. Even though Klee's watering can is but a small island in the blue surface, its radiance as a thing is more willful and bizarre than anything in an Impressionist work. Something almost alive permeates the material, it stirs, sits up, so to speak, changes form at its next encounter; in short, it is active. In negative terms this means that the painter distorts objects without doing violence to them. Might it not also be said that he liberates them by relieving them of their hard-edged boundaries?

Distortion is the price that has to be paid for the living unity. Art theory accounts for deformation as the supplanting of a perceived image by a represented image. Doesn't this mean only that one authority

is substituted for another? That whereas the artist formerly had to come to terms with a ready-made external world, now he must find the prefiguration of his work in a represented image? For our part, we believe that what actually takes place is something else. Klee's relationships of forms do not lean on the crutches of any conscious ideational program, do not stem from any sort of advance planning. Rather, they are surprising temptations that emerge directly—often without being sought—from the gamut of possibilities the creative act itself opens up. It is incumbent upon the artist to seek out such temptations, to go along with them wherever they may lead, finally to pick out from among the potential metamorphoses a suitable one and to realize it.

Current opinion still sees in the Expressionist artist a man "possessed," compelled to create by some elemental psychic urge. If this were the case, if the painter were so entirely at the mercy of unconscious powers, his caprices and distortions would be justified by extra-artistic motives. It seems to this writer that such an interpretation underestimates what used to be called artistic insight, with which artists of our own century are also endowed. It pays too little heed to the dialogue imposed on the painter by his artistic means, a dialogue quite possibly more compelling than his dialogue with the world of experience. The artistic means send out teasing hints and suggestions—the artist begins by letting himself be seduced by them, but soon turns this seduction (or "possession") to his own advantage. First "possessed" by the adventure of form, he becomes its master when he settles upon one particular formal possibility and takes possession of *it*. This is how Klee worked.

VI

Garden Still Life with Watering Can has the freshness and spontaneity of a child's first step—it breaks new artistic ground. This is why it has seemed to us particularly apt for revealing what is original in the pictorial structure of Expressionism. Everything is there already, but still *in nuce*, so to speak, in larval form, tuned to a single pitch, more presentiment than self-confident certainty. It lets us track down the new elements at their roots, in their first seeds. It would be wrong, however, to regard this watercolor as a standard by which to measure all the other, more obvious conquests of Expressionism. We must not be tempted to contrast its muted understatement with the rhetorical exaggerations and posterlike simplifications characteristic of many other Expressionist works. At the same time, it should be pointed out that the "shriek in the night" and the extravagantly bold gesture are no one's exclusive property. Expressionism also includes many a playful metamorphosis, and these may be more effective than more provoking tactics in unhinging the rationalist vision of the world.

Scientific terminology is no help in describing the formal processes referred to here and their results, the symbiotic formal relationships. We shall avoid speaking of "animation," for this term seems to apply to but one aspect of the problem. Though it takes into account the modifications to be observed in the things, it leaves out the interaction of forces between them. Moreover, it neglects—and this is its crucial defect—physical components in favor of psychic ones.

23

For this reason we are proposing another term, which does justice to both. It is to be found in Rilke's poetry, or, more accurately, it owes its evocative meaningfulness to this poet. Thanks to him it is adequate to the dimensions of our theme. The term is *Fühlung* (feeling, or spiritual rapport). This is the formula or catchword we have been looking for to define the nodal point where the various Expressionisms come together and from which every variation in their formal idiom derives.

As used here, the term stands for a reciprocal awareness which may range from a reticent exchange of pleasantries to orgiastic fusion. Because of its dialectical ambiguity it may serve as a key to the Expressionist experience as a whole. More than a century ago Ludwig Feuerbach wrote, no less rightly than naïvely: "We feel not only stones and different woods, not only flesh and bones, we also feel feelings. . . . In other words, not only outer reality, but also inner realities, not only the flesh but also the spirit, not only the thing but also the self are objects of the senses. That is why all things can be perceived by the senses, if not directly, then indirectly, if not with the coarse, vulgar senses, then with the cultivated senses." This idea alludes to the cipher-character of the work of art, to which we shall come back.

Consequently, spiritual rapport can be called forth by physical contact, but it can also develop along paths of sensibility without a visible partner. It is the now reticent, now eloquent intercourse between forms; it is the interaction between giving and receiving. The need to receive, to take in the world, is counterbalanced by the need to spend oneself, the desire to flow into the world and lose oneself in it. The Expressionist is at once introvert and extrovert, seeks to draw all things to him and to give himself to all things. From this point of view there is no apter interpretation of Expressionism than Kokoschka's "message from the I to the Thou." The message may be whispered, stammered, proudly affirmed, or shouted. It is addressed to the loved one, to men of good will, to the wretched of the earth, to the anonymous many, to nature both great and small, to plants, animals, and things.

But the relationship is a two-way one. The artist gives back to the objects of his love the message that his creative receptivity (skeptics will call it indiscretion) has wormed out of them.

VII

Of the various levels of expression the artist calls upon in this process, a few of the most important are represented in the present selection. Each involves a particular code system that theoretically permits the viewer two approaches. Either he may take the work of art for a message it is up to him to decode, or he may take it for a demonstration of the artist's prior decoding. The viewer who is attracted by the mystery will take the first approach, the viewer who is attracted by the revelation will take the second. Both expectations are justified, for the Expressionist work is Janus-faced. This dual aspect of the artistic message is not a discovery of our century, but it had to be rediscovered after a long period of illusionistic rationalism which tended to confine the artist to a routine "reading" of reality. The range of expressive possibilities tested by Expressionism had a lot to do with recovering a sense of the multiple meanings a work of art holds out to us.

Klee handles the reciprocal dialogue of things hesitantly, with delicacy and lyrical discretion. Kirchner's exultant orgy of color makes the banal big-city scene look as fresh as the first day of the Creation. John Marin transforms Fifth Avenue into a wild, ecstatic dance, with man and architecture forming one noisy, busy whole. Does this uproar denote an earthquake or the unleashing of some strange ritual of civilization? Does it herald the apocalyptic end of the world? These questions cannot be answered with perfect certainty, for there is no way to determine unequivocally on just which possible meaning the artist has put his accent.

Kandinsky's pandynamism goes still further. He merges heaven and earth. His thunderous, throbbing formulas of cosmic unity attest: "The world resounds. It is a cosmos of spiritually active beings." Yet is this watercolor a song of the world? Doesn't it show the world being smashed to pieces with monstrous dissonance? Kandinsky's cosmic hymn has overtones of disaster—possibly it contains an anticipation of the war. "Heroic departures! Ascensions! Tragic downfalls!" (J. R. Becher)—it is not only in the rhetoric of Expressionism that extremes come close to meeting. Kandinsky's more dramatic works were called "abstract," but the welter of line and color is only seemingly unrealistic. Not much would have to be added in the way of "objective" clues to make them readable, to relate them (for instance) to Otto Dix's *House at Angres* (p. 59). In Dix, too, the conventional, routine relations obtaining in the world of things have been shaken up. The war had taken over part of the work previously performed by the painter's imagination. Put out of joint by some machine-made violence, the wrecked house exhibits a tangible quality of aggression such as the human body discloses when cut open by the anatomist's knife. A wild, painful beauty emanates from this work, which is equally characteristic of the end and the beginning. This ambivalence transforms the heap of ruins into a metaphor of some primal experience. Kandinsky, Klee, Marc, and Kirchner were also on the track of some such experience, a chaos embodying the ferment, the fear, and the fruitfulness of life. Once again we encounter the fundamental Expressionist thesis: Nothing is for itself alone, all things are interconnected.

Art critics sometimes speak of Expressionist "panpsychism." Use of the term unfortunately leads to generalizations that overlook one fact: these painters never left out of account the tangible dimensions of the "felt" unity of all things. Nolde and Kokoschka painted many couples neither burdened with special problems nor psychologically differentiated. Rouault's *Woman with Feathered Hat* and Heckel's *Seated Child* (pp. 91, 75) are not disturbed by any desire, any longing. Physical existence is rendered in the former by vehement, energetic, colored curves, in the latter by a repose resembling still life. Nowhere is there indication of some peculiar "inwardness." Here the human figure is an anonymous creature reduced to type. In Heckel, who provides his watercolor with color notations, the *Fühlung* (or rapport) comes to no more than an attempt to test the impact of strong color contrasts. These figures would not be out of place in Derain's *Animated Landscape*. In this last, the rapport lies in the harmony of the bodies with nature's overwhelming fertility, a rejuvenating collective experience by which man hopes to free himself from the strictures and taboos of his civilization. "The world resounds"—here Kandinsky's dream, divested of its cosmic lines of force, has become unequivocal reality in the radiant here and now.

27

◁ ERNST LUDWIG KIRCHNER

VIII

The foregoing observations suggest a further line of inquiry into the Expressionist attitude toward reality. How did these artists stand in relation to their contemporaries? To what extent did their aspiration to create a "human culture" imply criticism of the tension-charged reality in which they lived? In what way, if at all, do their pictures (we shall not go into other testimonies they left) exhibit awareness of crisis in European civilization, social conflict, and the dynamics of a new age of scientific technology?

Unlike the Futurists and the Constructivists, the Expressionists were not admirers of technological civilization, but they were also far from the burlesque cynicism of the Dadaists at the expense of the middle-class world. Neither flatly negative nor wholeheartedly positive in their attitudes, they were in point of fact very consistent. These artists rejected the hypocritical morality, the functional rationalism, and the stifling conventions of their contemporaries—therein they expressed a critical aloofness. But in the same contemporary world they also saw the continuing play of vital instincts and existential conflicts, in which, however repressed by modern civilization, age-old human and natural forces still manifested themselves. In trying to grasp these forces, the Expressionist artist pleaded for their elemental, primordial significance, but by no means rejected his environment. Rather, the latter helped him to create metaphors, provided him with a point to rise above, with the stuff to boil down to its essence.

The image of the world that meets these needs is that of myth. In myth lie the roots of that mode of experience which civilization has buried deep and which the Expressionist sets out to rediscover, however consciously or not. The connections between Expressionist art and myth are obvious. In his 1922 essay, "Die Begriffsformen im mythischen Denken" ("Concepts in Mythical Thought") Ernst Cassirer adduces as a constitutive feature of mythical thinking the fact that "where we are able at best to recognize a mere analogy or external likeness, it finds a true community of essence." The belief that "all the world's physical processes are linked by imperceptible transitions" was shared by the Expressionist artist. This is why he could postulate active forces and irrational empathic relationships, such as are familiar to us from the mythical view of the world.

Such interpretations of the world are essentially magical. "All magic," Cassirer tells us, "is rooted in the premise that, just as with similarities between things, so their mere physical juxtaposition, contact between them, conceals mysterious forces. Any two things that have had such contact are grown together forever after in magic oneness."

To be rooted in myth offers the artist a fresh grasp of a world whose platitudinous, superficial functionalism leaves him unsatisfied. Viewed as a symbolic recurrence of the eternal, the present takes on new dimensions, becomes many-layered and transparent, a paradigm of the *conditio humana*. The Expressionist urge to make everything meaningful searches out uncomplicated, elementary metaphors for primordial

29

human experiences. Myth supplies them, for in it are preserved the inexhaustible, lapidary, basic patterns of all our hopes and desires, dreams and defeats.

The return to myth expresses longing for a unitary, comprehensive, emotionally charged reality. This was the path Gauguin had already chosen. When he ran away from the hurry and bustle of civilization and shed the superficial formal knowledge of academic idealism, he hoped to strike new roots. In one of his last letters he mentions Antaeus, the giant who regained his strength whenever he touched Mother Earth: "*La terre, c'est notre animalité, croyez-le bien.*" Gauguin's legacy can be discerned wherever the Expressionists pay tribute to vital instincts, evoke a primordial existence—in Derain's *Animated Landscape*, in Nolde's *Stage Scene*, in Heckel, and in Kirchner.

Kokoschka's *Lovers with Cat* (p. 87) falls under this heading only up to a point. More powerful here than the certainty of bodily contact is the age-old uncertainty that shrouds relations between the sexes. The man seems to be trying to make his way into the restful existence of the woman, but his presence is unacknowledged, he remains on the margin, excluded. The arrangement of the figures goes back to Etruscan sarcophagi; psychologically, we might trace the male's insistence back to Titian's *Shepherd and Nymph* in the Kunsthistorisches Museum in Vienna.

The figures of the mythical world make primordial, significant gestures. These are the areas of form out of which the Expressionist, like Antaeus, would draw the simplicity and immediacy that European art lost in the course of the centuries when Renaissance aesthetics held sway. Probably this is what accounts for the tendency that led, logically enough, to a mythologizing of the picture's contents. In other words, the deliberately primitive formal language forces its scanty, barely differentiated connotative energy upon the contents. Archaicized and barbarized, it still gives off powerful shock effects today. In the shadowless innocence of his bacchanalian revel, Derain discovers an echo to his own provocatively artless handwriting (p. 55). In Kirchner's cityscape a paradisiac fertility wells up and spills over the sober co-ordinates of rational planning (p. 83). Marin raises the chaotic Fifth Avenue traffic to the power of some mythical metaphor of the Metropolis (p. 47). In 1910 Kandinsky seems to intend a vivid metaphor of the spiritual processes he saw taking place around him in one vast two-way movement: "1. Disintegration of the soulless materialistic life of the nineteenth century, i.e., the fall of what is regarded as the only formal support of the material world, the breaking apart and dissolution of its individual parts. 2. Building up of the psychic/spiritual life of the twentieth century, what we are experiencing now and has already begun to manifest itself, embodied in strong, expressive, specific forms. The two processes are the two sides of the so-called modern movement." They are also the two inseparably interwoven aspects of the watercolor reproduced in this book (p. 79).

IX

The fairytale is one of myth's offspring. "It is an absolute chaos and contains an infinity of relations and meanings." Friedrich Schlegel's definition points in two directions. It links the infinite wealth of relation-

ships on the one hand to the world of myth, and on the other to the universal unity from which the Expressionists draw their metaphors.

Chagall reveals this interconnection of all things by an act of religious superstition. To find out whether they will live or die in the coming year, the Jews hold a chicken (men a rooster, women a hen) over the prayer book on Yom Kippur eve (p. 71). Man sees his own fate prefigured in that of the fowl.

Klee's night-blue landscape (p. 63) takes us entirely into the realm of the marvelous and the fairytale, and this is the locale, too, of Marc's *Three Fabulous Animals* (p. 103). The two works conjure up a harmony which man, excluded from immediate participation, gains the right to experience only temporarily, through the work of art.

> But in thy mysterious beasts,
> Radiating the same spirit from moist dark eyes,
> Thou wert my equal, forest!
>
> O, to be thy creature,
> Nothing but a vein in the earth,
> The butterfly a mottled drop of sun,
> And feel the strong blood
> Of slender foxes in a nearby bush:
> To be wholly love and brotherly peace!
>
> In thy mysterious beasts thou wert hallowed to me
> And I gave myself to thee,
> Dissolved in mists of desire!
>   (Iwan Goll, "Forest")

On the borderline of the fairytale is *Battling Fish* (p. 95), which Max Ernst painted in the trenches in 1917. (Does he allude to the big fish in the Bible, which devour the smaller?) Among the fairly numerous denizens in the category of "fabulous animals," they represent the possibilities of an art at once polyvalent and comic. Compared with the solemn simplicity of Marc's stylized animals, these fish are artfully constructed, sly, hybrid creatures. A certain roguishness relates them to Klee, but the mocking wit of the Dadaist and the mythologizing of the Surrealists are also anticipated. The watercolor documents a turning point of symptomatic significance; the credulous pathos of the Expressionist is put in question by being tinged with irony.

X

The dream is the fluid state of mind in which we all share the experience of the Expressionists that all things are bound up together. In the dreamer, who nightly produces his own world of myth and fairytale,

32

the artist sees a man who, like himself, undertakes to remake the world from experiential co-ordinates into an unlimited system of irrational relationships.

Picasso's *Brooding Woman* (p. 99) is such a creature. She derives from the series of pictures of figures seated at cheerless café tables, whose listless immobility had been depicted first by Degas and Toulouse-Lautrec. Latent in them and bound up with their immediate environment was a symbolic statement concerning the forlornness of the human condition. Picasso goes further: Renouncing all reference to time or place, refraining from social comment, he sets out to lay bare the prototype. This figure has something of the threatening passivity of the sphinx lying in wait for her victims, yet at the same time is imprisoned in her own mystery. In the hazy colors enveloping her, the brush finds a many-layered metaphor for the onrushing images of daydream, the total uncertainty and insecurity of being alone. (In much the same way, Picasso mythologizes the couple in the drawing on page 97, in whose timelessness we recognize the model of Christ with his favorite disciple, John.)

Compared with the flood of color playing around this figure like a manifold reflection of the temptations to which it is prey, Schiele's *Sleeping Girl (The Artist's Sister Gerda)* (p. 51) appears completely sheltered. But the comparison is deceptive. Looked at by itself, the figure betrays the dangers threatening it. The girl's body is not relaxed in sleep, but frozen, as though under a spell. The contour paraphrases a single theme: fragility. Since we do not know the nature of the body's surroundings, we are tempted to define them negatively as the void. Can there be bodily rest in the void, or is this sleep to be interpreted as an in-between state that bespeaks man's tragic rootlessness—anything but his freedom?

The stiff folds in which the garment is arranged are as vulnerable as the fragile outlines of arms, fingers, and facial features. The impression of weakness is corroborated by the large area given over to the hair. Its colors suggest dying embers and, echoing the lips, evoke autumn. The half-submerged profile, the forbidding gesture of the hand, and the severe clothing—all evince inaccessibility. Yet the posture and the palely glowing colors betray the secret that such modesty is ready to surrender. The desire this figure arouses and embodies is of the kind that Robert Musil described in his diary around 1900 as *"Herbstzeitlosfarbige Sinnlichkeiten"*: "a sensuality giving off the colors of the autumn crocus."

XI

We have related the areas of Expressionist experience to myth, fairytale, and dream. All three terms denote withdrawal from the ordinary, matter-of-fact world to one oriented toward ideal or romantic values. As we indicated from the outset, the shift has manifested itself in many spheres of artistic endeavor, intellectual life, and ideological world views. Their polyphonic intersection includes many creative and destructive possibilities, and constitutes one of the most fertile (and most fearful) impulses that the late nineteenth century passed on to the new one. We know today that irrationalism paved the way for what Karl Kraus called *Irrnationalismus*—nationalism run amok.

34

The voice of the Expressionists, beginning with Van Gogh, Gauguin, and Munch, is but one of a number that were raised all over Europe demanding a more intensive symbolic representation of reality, "greater depth, imagination, feeling for the human spirit." Expressionist painting represents the radical wing of this Europe-wide movement. Still to be inquired into is the exact character of this radicalism.

Intellectually and formally it is possible to define fairly accurately the point where the Expressionists, having advanced beyond their own beginnings, left the well-trodden, approved paths leading toward "greater depth." What direction did they pursue instead? Initially, their position was one of rejection. Before proclaiming new and wide-ranging freedoms they went through a phase of spiritual reappraisal and return to sober forms. They turned their backs on a public that thought in terms of prestige and cultural symbols; they distrusted the aesthetic façade designed to fill the burgher's need for edification in leisure moments and a feeling of security. They had no use for the academic humanism which clings to a Platonic harmony of the good, the true, and the beautiful; they were enemies of the fictitious values of the Establishment. Conscious of the crisis in European civilization, they denounced ready-made experience and the spiritual trash consumed by the "cultural Philistine," whom Hofmannsthal in 1893 defined as "the product of high-school, newspaper, and encyclopedia culture."

To these artistic and social criticisms, Central Europe added one of its own. The specifically German "fear of coming in contact with reality" resulted, in the Wilhelmian era, in "confining all spiritual values to the airtight box of inwardness and the correlative surrender of all real and public life to un- and anti-spiritual powers" (Max Scheler). The Expressionists took their stand against this ivory-tower "inwardness." From this stemmed their eloquence, their persuasive insistence, their "agitated" celebration of life; they drew their own strength from the vital instincts. Their art stood proudly "outside" all specially protected aesthetic private preserves.

Their success, however, was not due solely to their holding such principles. The Expressionist battles may have been fought on the battlefield of theory and ideals, but their victory was won by solid artistic accomplishment. The value of their work is not determined by exuberance or purity of feeling, not even by the authenticity and spontaneity they so strenuously searched for, but by the degree of success with which their venture in form is brought off. They broke with all the clichés of bourgeois traditionalism: not only with the pallid slickness of academicism, but also with the "tyranny of Divisionism" (Matisse), the playful elegance of Art Nouveau, the self-indulgent virtuosity of the Secessionists and the Post-Impressionists. In short, they broke with every mode of expression that made a show of cultivation or craftsmanship for its own sake.

Admirers of the most forthright authenticity, the Expressionists set against well-worn traditional values other values: ". . . the new and surprising, the colorful, adventurous, and bizarre, the wild and vehement . . . grotesque figures . . . swift transitions—opulent forms, harsh contrasts, dazzling lights, lyrical pathos." This catalogue of Expressionist idioms was drawn up by Schiller in the late eighteenth century, in his

37

◁ FRANZ MARC

Letters on the Aesthetic Education of Mankind. Of course, Schiller's list is one of condemnation—to him these values represent the most crude and primitive manifestations of the aesthetic instinct. "The sensual instinct with its willfulness and untamed desires" has always to be surmounted. It has long been part of the idealistic gospel of beauty, with its faith in progress, to condemn any "regression" to the "barbaric" origins of art as purely and simply "crudity of taste." The epigones of classical aesthetics mistrust every kind of primitivism; every recall of the "heartiness, solidity, and robustness of bygone times" strikes them as an anachronistic return to the "rudeness of early customs." It affronts their austere conception of beauty to exhibit any great wealth of imaginative invention. The sober rules of rationalism demand, rather, a beauty accessible to all.

So, at last, we must recognize in what quarter the prehistory of the Expressionist movement lies: in primitivism and irrationalism. Its origins go back much further than to mere nay-saying to the "official" culture of the day. Expressionism restored to their true rank the creative forces which Jean Paul's "Vorschule der Ästhetik" ("Elementary Principles of Aesthetics")—written ten years after Schiller's essay—assigned to the all-powerful faculty of the imagination. That term is sadly underrated today—it sounds naïve, insufficiently pretentious. All the same, it denotes an essential feature of Expressionism. For Jean Paul, the imagination is nature's "hieroglyphic alphabet," which "welds all parts into wholes (whereas the other faculties, like experience itself, merely tear out pages from the book of nature) and all pieces of the world into worlds; it totalizes all things, including the infinite All." This is the secret of that rapport which runs the gamut from the nearest to the remotest to unite all things in one mighty stream of interrelationships. This was the royal road Expressionist art took.

List of Watercolors and Drawings

41 Maurice de Vlaminck: *Head of Woman.* c. 1905. Original woodcut. $4 \times 6^1/_4''$. Private collection (Photo: Bildarchiv W. Arntz, Haag, Upper Bavaria)

43 Maurice de Vlaminck: *The Village.* 1910–20. Watercolor and gouache. $14^1/_8 \times 20^1/_8''$. Private collection, Stuttgart

45 John Marin: *Woolworth Building and Vicinity.* 1914. Pencil. $9^1/_2 \times 7^1/_2''$. Downtown Gallery, New York (Photo: O. Baker, New York)

47 John Marin: *Movement—Fifth Avenue.* 1912. Watercolor. $16^1/_2 \times 13^1/_2''$. Art Institute of Chicago (Alfred Stieglitz Collection)

49 Egon Schiele: *The Artist and His Model.* 1910. Pencil. $20^1/_8 \times 12^7/_8''$. Albertina, Vienna

51 Egon Schiele: *Sleeping Girl (The Artist's Sister Gerda).* 1911. Pencil, watercolor, and gouache. $17^5/_8 \times 12^1/_4''$. Albertina, Vienna *missing 11/30/77*

53 André Derain: *Barges.* 1905. Pen drawing. $17^3/_4 \times 13''$. Galerie Berggruen, Paris

55 André Derain: *Animated Landscape (Bacchanal).* 1906. Watercolor. $8^1/_2 \times 12^5/_8''$. Private collection, Paris

57 Otto Dix: *Man Falling.* 1918. Black chalk and tusche. $16 \times 15''$. Galerie im Erker, Saint Gall, Switzerland (Photo: G. Boesch, Saint Gall)

59 Otto Dix: *House at Angres.* 1917. Gouache. $11^3/_8 \times 11^1/_4''$. Saarland Museum, Saarbrücken, Germany

61 Paul Klee: *Garden Still Life with Watering Can.* 1910. Watercolor. $5^3/_8 \times 5''$. Municipal Gallery in the Lenbachhaus, Munich (Photo: J. Blauel, Munich)

63 Paul Klee: *Gardens by Night.* 1918. Gouache. $10 \times 4^7/_8''$. Collection Lady Nika Hulton, London

65 Emil Nolde: *Skaters.* 1908. Black tusche, brush, and pen. $8^1/_2 \times 10^1/_4''$. Ada and Emil Nolde Foundation, Seebüll, Germany

67 Emil Nolde: *Stage Scene.* Berlin, 1910–11. Watercolor. $11^3/_4 \times 8^7/_8''$. Ada and Emil Nolde Foundation, Seebüll, Germany

69 Marc Chagall: *Full Moon.* c. 1911. Tusche. Private collection

71 Marc Chagall: *Eve of Yom Kippur.* 1912. Gouache. $12^5/_8 \times 10^5/_8''$. Marlborough Fine Art Ltd., London

73 Erich Heckel: *Woman Resting.* 1913. Pencil. $17^3/_4 \times 13^1/_4''$. Roman Norbert Ketterer, Campione d'Italia (Photo: H. F. Wülferode, Hanover)

75 Erich Heckel: *Seated Child.* 1910. Watercolor and pencil. $13^1/_2 \times 17^1/_2''$. Private collection, Germany

77 Wassily Kandinsky: *Study for "Improvisation."* 1915. Pen drawing. $8^1/_4 \times 5^1/_2''$. Private collection, Paris

79 Wassily Kandinsky: *Improvisation.* 1915. Watercolor. $8^3/_4 \times 4^1/_2''$. Private collection, Paris

81 Ernst Ludwig Kirchner: *Streetwalkers.* 1911. Reed pen, brush, tusche wash. $18^7/_8 \times 14^5/_8''$. Private collection, Düsseldorf (Photo: Wiemann, Recklinghausen)

83 Ernst Ludwig Kirchner: *The Stübelallee (Stübel Avenue).* 1912. Watercolor. $13^1/_2 \times 17^3/_8''$. Collection Roman Norbert Ketterer, Campione d'Italia

85 Oskar Kokoschka: *Birth of Christ.* 1910. Tusche and pen over preliminary pencil drawing. $8 \times 9^1/_2''$. Kunstmuseum, Bern (Nell Walden Collection) (Photo: H. Stebler, Bern)

87 Oskar Kokoschka: *Study for "Lovers with Cat."* 1917. Watercolor. $12^7/_8 \times 16^3/_4''$. Private collection, Germany

89 Georges Rouault: *Mau-Mau.* 1914. Tusche, brush drawing. $10^1/_2 \times 7^7/_8''$. Musée d'Art Moderne de la Ville de Paris (Photo: Y. Chevalier, Paris)

91 Georges Rouault: *Woman with Feathered Hat.* 1909. Ink and watercolor. $10^5/_8 \times 8^5/_8''$. Private collection, Paris

93 Max Ernst: *Paris Street.* 1912. Watercolor. $13^3/_8 \times 17^3/_8''$. Städtische Kunstsammlungen, Bonn

95 Max Ernst: *Battling Fish.* 1917. Watercolor. $6 \times 8^5/_8''$. Collection the artist

97 Pablo Picasso: *Couple.* 1904. Charcoal drawing. $13^1/_2 \times 10''$. Galerie Berggruen, Paris

99 Pablo Picasso: *Brooding Woman.* 1904(?). Watercolor. $10^1/_2 \times 14^1/_2''$. Museum of Modern Art, New York (Donated by Mr. and Mrs. Werner E. Josten)

101 Franz Marc: *Abstract Composition with House and Garden.* 1914. Tusche. $8^5/_8 \times 6^1/_2''$. Private collection

103 Franz Marc: *Three Fabulous Animals.* 1913. Tempera. $18 \times 15^1/_2''$. Hannema-De Stuers Foundation, Heino, Holland

marin

49

1910 47

Erich Heckel

85

1914/1   Franz Gartu

Nachlass Franz Marc bestätige Maria Marc